P9-DER-007

Just Mutts

Just Mutts

A Tribute to The Rogues of Dogdom

Text by Steve Smith and Gene Hill

WILLOW CREEK PRESS
MINOCQUA, WISCONSIN

Design and production by Patricia Bickner Linder.

ISBN 1-57223-042-8

Second printing, 1997

Published by WILLOW CREEK PRESS,
PO Box 147, Minocqua, WI 54548

For more information on Willow Creek Press books,
call 1-800-850-9453.

Library of Congress Cataloging-in-Publication Data

Printed in Canada

Smith, Steve, 1947-
Just mutts : a tribute to the rogues of dogdom / text by Steve Smith.
p. cm.
ISBN 1-57223-042-8 (alk. paper)
1. Mutts (Dogs) 2. Mutts (Dogs)--Pictorial works. I. Title.
SF426.2.S59 1996
636.7--dc20 96-35742
CIP

PHOTOGRAPHY CREDITS

Kent & Donna Dannen, pp. 2, 12, 18L, 30R, 37R, 49R, 50M, 77.
Robert Cushman Hayes, pp. 5, 18UR, 87, 113.
Uli Degwert/Langone Studio, pp. 6, 92.
Bill Buckley/The Green Agency, pp. 9, 26, 38, 41, 43, 47, 48R, 49L, 68, 78, 85, 86, 90, 96, 101, 103.
Robert Sisk/The Green Agency, pp. 11, 32R, 51, 74R.
Bob Firth/Firth Photobank, pp, 13, 55, 57UL, 61, 89.
Terry Wild, pp. 14, 58L, 70, 73L, 79, 81, 83L, 95, 110.
Walter Chandoha, pp. 15L, 25L, 29L, 46R, 48L, 50L, 50R, 53, 54L, 57M, 59, 67, 69, 71L, 73R, 74L, 80, 83R, 93, 102, 105, 111, 115, 116.
Gale Zucker, pp. 16, 20, 21, 88, 91.
Richard Hamilton Smith, p. 17L.
Dale C. Spartas, pp. 17R, 33, 82, 84, 104, 112, 117, 120, 126.
Jane Lidz/F-Stock, p. 18UR.
Morning Star Photo, pp. 18BR, 24R, 25R, 27L, 58R.
Jeff Richter, pp. 22, 23.
John Schafer, pp. 24L, 30L, 32L.
Pete Maina, p. 27R.
Frank Siteman/Omni-Photo, p. 28.
Arni Katz/Unicorn Stock Photos, p. 29R.
Bonnie Sue Rauch, p. 31.
H.J. Schmidt/The Green Agency, pp. 34, 35.
Caroline Wood/F-Stock, p. 36L.
Lance Krueger, p. 36R.
David Stoecklein/F-Stock, p. 37L.
Michael Montgomery, p. 45.
Aneal Vohra/Unicorn Stock Photos, p. 46L
Judd Cooney, p. 52.
Kirk Anderson, p. 54R, 118.
Diane Ensign/The Green Agency, p. 56.
Vision Impact, pp. 57BR, 94, 106, 107, 108, 114.
Chuck Wyrostok/Appalight, p. 60.
Paul Murphy/Unicorn Stock Photos, pp. 71R, 76.
Tommy Dodson/Unicorn Stock Photos, p. 75.
Steve Bly/F-Stock, p. 72.
Lon Lauber, p. 124.

Contents

INTRODUCTION

Behold the Mongrel Hordes

Mutts are different from other dogs. Truth be told, they are more like people than they are animals. Mutts look at the world through squinted eyes, eyes that have seen it all, too many times. They are impressed by little; canine Bogarts, a sneer on their lips, they have their own sense of fair play, of dignity. The heart of a mutt is the heart of a lion, showing the hybrid vigor that makes him stronger than the sum of his component parts.

If you travel far enough south in Mexico, you will encounter the elemental edition of "dog" schlepping about the sleepy little villages with their dirt streets and friendly folk.

These dogs are, almost uniformly, about fourteen to sixteen inches at the shoulder, have pointy ears that flop over, and tails that they carry high, curving over their backs. They are sort of yellow-brown in color, and their fur is very short.

They are the results of generations of the most non-selective breeding you can imagine, and they show us what *Canis familiaris* looks like when left alone and to his own devices. And devices they have. These mendicants are the animal world's answer to the street children of Sparta, turned loose at a young age to fend for themselves, with the survivors supposedly making the best, most resourceful soldiers for the city-state's army.

Those kids couldn't hold a candle to the mutts of Mexico when it comes to swiping a free meal, finding an out-of-the-way place to snooze away a hot afternoon, or spawning an ever-smarter race of freebooters.

Dr. Jim Hall of Medford, Oregon, a friend of long standing, recently made me aware of the contributions mutts are making for the hearing-impaired. Doc told me about Dogs for the Deaf, a non-profit institution that trains and places dogs with the ability to be their masters' ears. These guys notify their "partners" when the phone rings, when the oven timer goes off, when someone's at the door – a whole list of things. Doc says that unlike guide dogs for the blind, these hearing-assist pooches are mostly crossbreeds – mutts, ladies and gentlemen. It appears that they catch on just as quickly as the purebred dogs, and they're readily available from animal shelters. And, the cost of acquisition and training for these dogs runs about one-third of what it does to train the purebred dogs to do their jobs as guide dogs. Only goes to prove that mutts know how to get by on a shoestring – and get the job done.

But that's not any surprise to those of us who have spent a lot of time hanging out with dogs whose lineage is even more suspect than our own. Their power to reason, and their powers of dedication to a task, can be at times staggering – and often just as misdirected as those of their human pals.

When I was a kid, we lived for a while in Washington state, hard against the boundary of Mt. Rainier National Park. We had some family friends who had a mutt named Spike.

Spike was about as nondescript as you could imagine. Depending on how the light hit him, you could see some hound, cocker spaniel, Labrador retriever, and border collie. And some other stuff.

Anyway, Spike, like most of us, had a weakness, and his was what us kids called "whistle pigs": hoary marmots. Specifically, he liked to fight with them. I never knew if he intended to kill one and eat it, but my guess is that he never got the chance, because every time he wandered off into the mountains to look for a little action, the whistle pigs would gang up and beat the living snot out of him.

He'd come back in a couple days, limping into his family's yard, drawn and bedraggled with some of the stuffings hanging out. He was a sight. Normally, one eye was squinted shut from deep scratches. His nose would be bleeding, a paw or two was chewed up where it looked like the whistle-pigs gnawed on him. One ear, apparently on his blind side, was always shredded, and toward the end essentially wasn't there anymore.

Spike would hobble up the back steps to his box in the utility room, flop down on his comfy blanket, and sleep for a day. Then he'd rouse enough to accept food and the bandages and ointments and creams and disinfectants his family showered on him. After a week of this type of treatment, he'd be seen in the yard, catching the sun's rays in the afternoon. Two weeks later, he'd be gone. Back to the mountains. Back to the whistle pigs. Some guys never get enough.

We moved away before I found out how things eventually wound up, while Spike was off on one of his expeditions. I hope he finally won one.

These, then, are the mutts, the guys and gals who brighten our days, make us laugh, and aim to please. *Just Mutts* honors them and their singular way of life.

– Steve Smith
Traverse City, Michigan

A Rogues' Gallery

Or, How to Tell a Mutt from
A Fancy-pants Purebred

▶ Purebred Golden Retriever
▼ Golden Retriever Mix

Generations of linebreeding and inbreeding have yielded the gorgeous coat and happy brown eyes of the golden retriever. That same genetic encoding stamps dim-witted characteristics.

Mutts, on the other hand, are the haphazard result of accidental breedings: countless random couplings and back-alley trysts—because it seemed like a good idea at the time. The results include a variety of colors, shapes, sizes, and markings. While the purebred is boringly uniform, mutts collectively offer a dazzling viewing experience – a gallery of modern art as opposed to a plate block of postage stamps, each monotonously identical to the rest.

ROTTINI

◀ Purebred Newfoundland

▶ Not Purebred Newfoundlands

Purebreds are known for their well-groomed coats. Mutts, on the other hand, are usually unkempt, their coats prone to attracting dirt, dust, and critters. Give a mutt a fancy haircut, and *voila!* He or she has been instantly transformed, before your very eyes, into . . . a mutt with a fancy haircut.

9·94
9·92
teléfono público
EL SIGLO

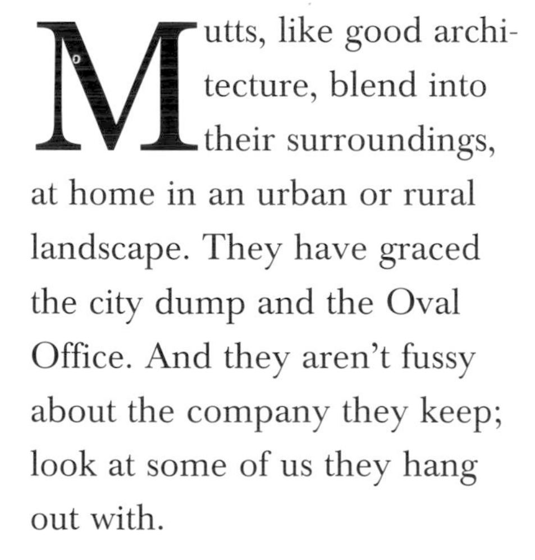

Mutts, like good architecture, blend into their surroundings, at home in an urban or rural landscape. They have graced the city dump and the Oval Office. And they aren't fussy about the company they keep; look at some of us they hang out with.

There is similarity, however. One common attribute of this band of hoboes is a set of intelligent eyes behind a bristle-brush mustache. If you call Central Casting and ask for a mutt, they'll send you a pooch in desperate need of a shave.

Close to purebred, but no cigar. "Mutt" doesn't necessarily carry with it a stigma. After all, when America was designated "the great melting pot," that was just another way of saying, "Hey, we're *all* mutts."

Instead, "mutt" can connote independence, self-esteem, a devil-may-care attitude, a level of canine swagger and shrewdness that sets this particular lad or lady apart from the blue-blooded, freshly-bathed, skittish, yappy, perfumed little lap dog with the pedigree a mile long and the savvy of your average beach stone.

Mutts are a working-class lot. They tend the store, mind the farm, keep neighborhood pests at bay, protect the homestead, and generally lend a paw where they think they can help out.

Mutts, the most democratic of creatures, exhibit patience and tolerance in equal, admirable portions. This comes from the ability to be able to determine which side of their bread carries the butter. "You've got to go along to get along."

Anyone who has one knows that the mutt's itinerant nature makes him want to go where you go, when you go there. Try to get away without them – it can't be done . . . A mutt that takes six months to (sort of) learn the meaning of "no" will, in something just under twenty seconds, soak in forever the fact that jingling keys mean a free ride somewhere, and it doesn't matter too much where.

DELTA
4x4

Most mutts live by the precepts of the tips contained in *The Freeloader's Guide to Life in the Soft Lane*. The Preamble states: "If you're going to be a mutt, be a good one. The life of a freeloading vagabond can be greatly enhanced by following a few, simple guidelines. These can be modified for your personal use and adapted as needed."

Tip Seventeen states, "If you've been out carousing all night with the fellows and you come wandering in the next morning, feign a limp. This will allay punishment and get you some sympathy. You were brave, see, to fight unknown perils and obstacles to make your way back to the homestead because your family needs you."

Brown Dog

by Gene Hill

Lately, there's been an upsurge in the popularity of what's called the "versatile hunting dog." The term covers several breeds, all European in origin. Now, while I'm not knocking any claims about them as such, I'd like to point out that this country has had such a dog for longer than I can remember. It's not really a breed; it's more of a type. I had one when I was a kid, and nearly everyone else I knew had one at some time or another. You might call it a "brown dog."

Brown dogs are not really all brown. Some run a little orange in the coat and others have a pronounced grayish, but lackluster, cast. Still, common brown is the predominant shade. The hair may be sort of long, though not necessarily, and can be either smooth or rough or in-between. They have a peculiar three quarter sideways gait as if the front wheels are out of alignment, and they tend to use only one back leg at a time, resting one or the other alternately unless an emergency occurs requiring full power.

No farm can be said to be properly run unless there's a brown dog in some position of authority. They will herd cows and pigs, keep the chickens out of the house garden, and keep the area free from skunks – which accounts, in large measure, for their rather distinct odor.

No boy can be properly raised without one. I think it was Robert Benchley who once remarked, "Every boy should have a dog. It teaches him to turn around three times before lying down." Brown dogs do a great deal more than that. They provide excuses for adventures, teach him how to whistle loud and clear, improve his throwing arm, and, most important, instill in him the incredible responsibility that comes with being loved unquestioningly, totally, and irrevocably.

Brown dogs are famous for their nonchalant, sophisticated attitudes. They have an attitude of preoccupation. Mine would stop now and then and stare into middle distance, as if pondering some crucial question for a minute or so. Then, having resolved it to his satisfaction, he'd shake his head as though wishing he could impart this gem of knowledge to me, but somehow feel it would be wasted or, more likely, that I simply would not understand its value.

A brown dog will tolerate a boy's family but will not get too involved. If the boy is absent, say during school days, he will mope around or curl up close to where the master will first appear upon coming home, and wait. If there are things he has to attend to, rounds to make or whatever, never doubt that the sound of the school bus will fall on his ears first and farthest away. When the owner of a brown dog I know went off to college, the dog would move out to the end of the lane about a day and a half before his pal was due home. How did he know? I haven't the foggiest idea. Since the boy's father didn't know when to expect him home either, it's even more mysterious – except that, if you're a brown dog, you're expected to know such things and it's your job to act on them.

Brown dogs are never trained in the common usage of words. They just figure out what has to be done and they do it. If you need someone to sit and listen to your problems, they'll lend a most sympathetic ear. If you're bursting with spring, they'll race up and down the brook with you and even walk a little taller when you bring mom the first sprigs of myrtle or watercress. I suspect they like summer best of all because everyone's home.

Brown dogs are very fond of parties: swimming hole picnics, hayrides, summer softball games, fireworks, bicycling, fishing trips, and camping out. They make good outfielders and lifeguards, and I wouldn't have dreamed of sleeping on the lawn without my brown dog to watch over me; nor would he have allowed it in the first place.

Most problems with brown dogs stem from their intelligence and unswerving desire to please. Mine went along with me and my first .22 to watch me get rid of a few groundhogs in one of the pastures. I suppose I shot two or three; I forget. But he got the idea that we wanted groundhogs, and nearly every day, all that summer, he brought one home. The problem was that he didn't bring them home immediately, but waited a day or so until they were

more impressive – in both size and smell. That little lesson wasn't lost to me either. I learned that there were certain outings to go on alone after that, especially when I was going to shoot snakes in the ice pond or around the place in the brook where we liked to swim. What would have happened if he had decided we wanted water snakes strung out on the porch? It still fills me with pangs of desperation.

One neighbor had to keep a chain around the kitchen icebox door after his brown dog learned to open and close it. It was a mystery where the food was going for a while, since he was smart enough not to take a lot or too big of a piece . . . just a small snack now and then to tide him over in the evening hours. Another had to tie the dog in the cellar or the barn if he felt he had to spank his son, and even then the dog would snarl a little at him for two or three days, as if to say he knew and didn't like the idea at all.

It's a shame that not everyone has a brown dog to help him over the rough spots, or to share that time of incredible wonder and discovery. A brown dog is a special gift we should have at a certain time of our life to round it out. A brown dog belongs to that time of life which was filled with dreams of what we see today as small things: slingshots, a first pocket knife of your very own, and hip boots; the little keys that opened the first doors to the treasures we now prize above price. Somehow brown dogs understand these things, and know how to share them.

I used to think, with pride overflowing, that my brown dog was mine. Now I know better. We never really own a dog as much as he owns us. Where he led I would follow without fear, and even now, remembering how he would curl up with his back against my bedroom door, I know again how it was to feel safe and protected from anything and anyone.

Once when I was very small and very sick my mother put him in bed with me against everyone's advice. "They need each other," she said, and that was that. She understood brown dogs and their peculiar magic.

It's getting about that time for another brown dog to come and live around the place. Sometimes I feel a strange cold draft at night. A brown dog would know just how to curl his back up against the door to keep it from troubling me.

Muttness

It's an Attitude

Muttness is tolerating an embarrassing situation with inherent dignity; it's conforming to a stereotype without apology or care; it's doing what you want to do when you want to do it, and doing what you *have* to do in order to keep the right folks happy.

It's spending a lot of the time on the outside looking in, waiting patiently for that special someone to come out so that life can, once again, move along. A mutt figures, "Hey, As long as I'm out here, I might as well make friends."

A lot of the waiting is in the car or The Big Guy's truck, where, since you're unsupervised, you can be submissive . . . indifferent . . . or downright hostile. It sort of depends on your mood that day.

"Muttness" is not, however, reserved only for those whose mother was a Heinz 57, and whose daddy was whatever wandered by, hopped the backyard fence, and wandered off again.

That's because the essence of muttness does not belong only to the beast of garbled ancestry. Ever caught your AKC champion Irish setter shredding the neighbor's garbage bags? Have you surprised your prize malamute munching on a mole he dug out of the flower bed? Or has your expensive Yorkshire terrier found that the smell he finds just right can only come from a leisurely roll in a little roadkill? If so, then you understand the concept.

Muttness is hanging out with their friends . . .

. . . or just hanging out, something of a mutt specialty.

Tip Number Six from *The Freeloaders Guide:* "It's easiest to get up on the good furniture when nobody's home. If your fur is dark colored, choose dark furniture; if it's light, stretch out on the light furniture. It will be days before they discover it, and your people operate under the misconception that they can't punish you unless they catch you in the act, otherwise you won't know why you're being punished. *Ha!* This is The Fraternity's Great, Unspoken Secret. Don't ever tell anyone the truth."

Tip Number Seven: "If you manage to get adopted by a family with existing pets, do your absolute, level best to get along with everything from the fluffy kitty to Lester the llama. If you can't get along with one another, the rule of 'last hired, first fired' applies."

Muttness is self-training. Because they weren't bred for specific purposes, such as pointing, trailing, or retrieving, mutts are free to pursue personal forms of self-expression.

Fred

by Gene Hill

Fred arrived late in the spring as if he had a long-standing appointment with us, or like an old and tired fellow looking for a friend to take him in for a bit until he was back on his feet again – nothing permanent, you understand, just a little while until the expected letter arrived, or a distant but well-to-do relative came to collect him and return him to the standard of living he was obviously accustomed to.

He was pathetically tired and listless for the first week or so; no doubt the journey had been long and arduous, beset with perils he had somehow, with pluck and wit, survived – no easy task for a rather small half-breed beagle more than a little done in by age and its nuisances.

At first the other dogs more or less ignored him and he seemed to prefer it that way. But as his condition improved and most of the aches and pains went away, he would join them in a few minutes of rolling around, then retire to his spot under the front porch and watch them.

Nor did he pay very much attention to me or anyone else in the family. He had the typical beagle disdain for coming when he was called – or perhaps he just didn't care for our calling him "Fred." Now and than he would want to be scratched or petted and would come to me and put his head against my foot and look away into some secret vision of his own for a few minutes. Then, having done his duty or satisfied some canine itch, he would wander off and stretch out by himself.

In deference to Fred's age, his refusal to come when called unless it was convenient, and my lack of interest in rabbit hunting, I left him alone to do as he pleased. I had put him in a wire run to force him to rest, and because of some sentimental reason or other, I had become rather attached to him and didn't want him taking off to start another journey of indefinite end and purpose. But after a couple of weeks, I set him free to wander around the house and yard. He seemed content to do just that; besides, he had a habit of digging holes in his area that were about ten inches wide and two feet deep, and I was afraid I'd step in one in the dark and snap an ankle.

After he'd been with us a couple of months, Fred actually began to act rather spry every so often. He had a little game he liked to play, and I can see him yet with his pet toy – an old leather gardening glove of mine – running and barking and throwing the glove up in the air and catching it, hoping that one of the other dogs would come and try to play catch with him. Sadly, they never seemed to express more than the most fleeting interest in Fred's glove, and after a minute or two of barking and throwing, he would give up and take his glove with him back under the porch.

Once a week or so Fred would disappear on a personal errand in the morning and be gone until almost dark; typical Beagle goings-on. But when, on one occasion, he didn't come home for a couple of days, I began to worry and started asking around the neighborhood for sightings of the old man. I was very much relieved to come home from work one night and see his gray muzzle poking out from near the front step. He was wet and bedraggled and just plain worn out, but he was back.

Any of us who has owned a dog that has taken a particular hold on our heart has dwelt on the unfairness of allotted time. It seems but an instant – or at best a couple of good years – that the puppy we so carefully carried home and placed on the rug by our bed has suddenly become a little dim of eye, a touch slow to get up in the morning, and more and more content to lay in some sunny spot. Somehow, even through the dozen dogs I've owned, I've never ceased to be surprised and a little hurt to discover that today Tippy or Ben or Judy doesn't race me to the door, but stands in the warm kitchen and merely follows me with eyes and heart.

You'd think, as I should have, that having Fred move in in his declining years would have made this understanding of the impermanence of things a little easier, but somehow it didn't. I knew Fred was old, but he seemed to be the type that might have been born old and would keep that curious dignity and charming wisdom for quite a time to come.

Fred finally formed some sort of obvious attachment to me. Needless to say, I had made every effort to spoil him. The best of the table scraps were delivered to the cavern under the porch, and I found that some of the work I usually did elsewhere could be done as easily on the front step where I could reach down and scratch his head for whatever comfort it was. At least it comforted me, and ever since then I am often consumed with the belief that one of the selfish reasons we get so attached to our dogs is the fact that they give us something to love and care for which is irreplaceable in our lives – a quiet, understanding, grateful being that is there when we feel the need to hold and love something warm, mute, and grateful. I would think of my teasing my daughters Patty or Jennifer about a room full of stuffed animals as I rolled on the lawn and played with old Fred, and I'd have to laugh at myself.

One of Fred's habits had been to come out from under the porch when I drove up to the house and then bark once or twice just enough to let me know he cared. He would never bark at anyone else; I was special.

Fred continued to have his restless side. His habit of stopping whatever he was doing and staring beyond whatever my normal eyes could see was always slightly unnerving, as if the dog were seeing ghosts or hearing sounds or musing on thoughts that were beyond sharing with me. He never let me really deep down inside; or believe that our relationship was anything more than a transient one; but that he was in the course of a journey that constantly tempted him to be on with it. Often I watched him pace slowly to the edge of the driveway and stare down the road, consider the alternatives, and slowly shaking his head, turn around and make his way back as if saying, "Not today, but perhaps tomorrow."

And that "tomorrow" finally came. I pulled into the driveway burdened by some large and small worries and needed someone to sit with and sort them out into piles of "not today, but perhaps tomorrow." Fred was always the perfect companion with whom to discuss this sort of thing. He would let me go on and on, knowing that this was the best way – to say nothing and let me work things out for myself. I went into the house, made myself a drink, and came out and sat on the front step. The emptiness of the little dusty hole was cavernous; no, it was more than that. By the time I had finished my glass of whiskey, I realized that it was final. Even the old glove was gone, and I could easily imagine Fred inching along, carrying his glove both as a reminder of where he'd been and as a symbol of total commitment to going on . . . all of his worldly possessions were with him; there was no need ever to turn back.

After a week of teasing myself, I rummaged

around in the barn and found the old lattice that I had taken out from the porch to paint and put it back as if to erase the sight of Fred's room; closing a door to a place I would rather not have anyone else see or use.

A few months passed. Fred had almost gone from my mind and I could sit on the porch with an evening glass and think about him more in terms of pleasure than remorse. In the overall, he had left on good terms, and the loss I felt was rather selfish on my part, and I'd come to see it like that. So I was not prepared for Fred's return in spirit or name when a man who worked for the county road crew stopped by one afternoon and asked me if I had a beagle who had recently disappeared. I said I did – in a way. He asked me if I knew what had become of him, and I said that I didn't. He then told me that he had found him, lying dead along the edge of the road, killed by a careless, uncaring driver. He had buried Fred, not knowing at the time that he was my dog.

I couldn't think of anything to say. I never could and still can't. Death has a way of affecting my mind for a while and I seem forever falling short of finding any way to take it all in and make sense of it. But after a minute or so, I thanked him for his kindness toward the dog and his courtesy of coming by. He asked me if I wanted to know who did it and I thought about that and, remembering a red rage I felt once during a long-ago war, I said I'd rather not know. He seemed a little surprised, but I didn't feel I wanted to explain; I didn't feel I could – I didn't understand it myself – it just sort of came out. He said, "Okay," in a way that embarrassed me, and got back in his truck. He started the motor, rolled the window down, and held out an old leather glove. "This yours?" he asked. I took it, wordlessly, and he drove off.

I went back and sat on the front step, trying not to think and not having much luck. My wife came out and asked who had stopped by in the truck. I couldn't say anything to her, but I held up the glove. "I'm glad to have that," she said and took it from me and pushed it under the lattice and went back into the house. She came back in a minute or two and handed me a glass and went away again.

I sat there and watched the sun go down, and off in the shallow part of the sky where the weakening yellow was being pushed back by the dark, I saw the evening star, and I made a wish.

A Day in the Life

*When each day is like
the last and the next, you
have to get creative.*

Since everyone knows the most important meal is breakfast, the day should start off with a good meal – most mongrels prefer cafeteria-style.

A good part of the day can be spent hanging around the house, further livened by trying to get out if you're in, or in if you're out. One's as good as the other.

. . . or you can kill a little time with a little freelance yowling – it's so endearing to the neighbors, after all, especially if they work nights.

Of course, children are a mutt's source of unending amusement and a first-class diversion. If it's summer vacation and everybody's home, life is good.

Tip Number Two: "Little kids very often have candy on their person; they also aren't very attentive. If you follow them around long enough, they'll swing a piece of it within reach, and then you can make your move. Caution: Make sure you don't nail the kid when you lunge or you'll find out the meaning of the phrase 'to lose one's happy home."

Then, of course, there's the side amusements of hanging out with one's best pal . . . a little tug-of-war . . . or rummaging through the trash to see if someone thoughtlessly tossed out a bone.

By the way, Tip Number Five: "If you have that overpowering urge to shred a newspaper, or tip over a garbage pail, make sure you do it off-campus – at the neighbor's. No sense rocking the boat at home. Besides, remember the Mutt's Rule: *'If they don't see you do it, they can't prove it.'"*

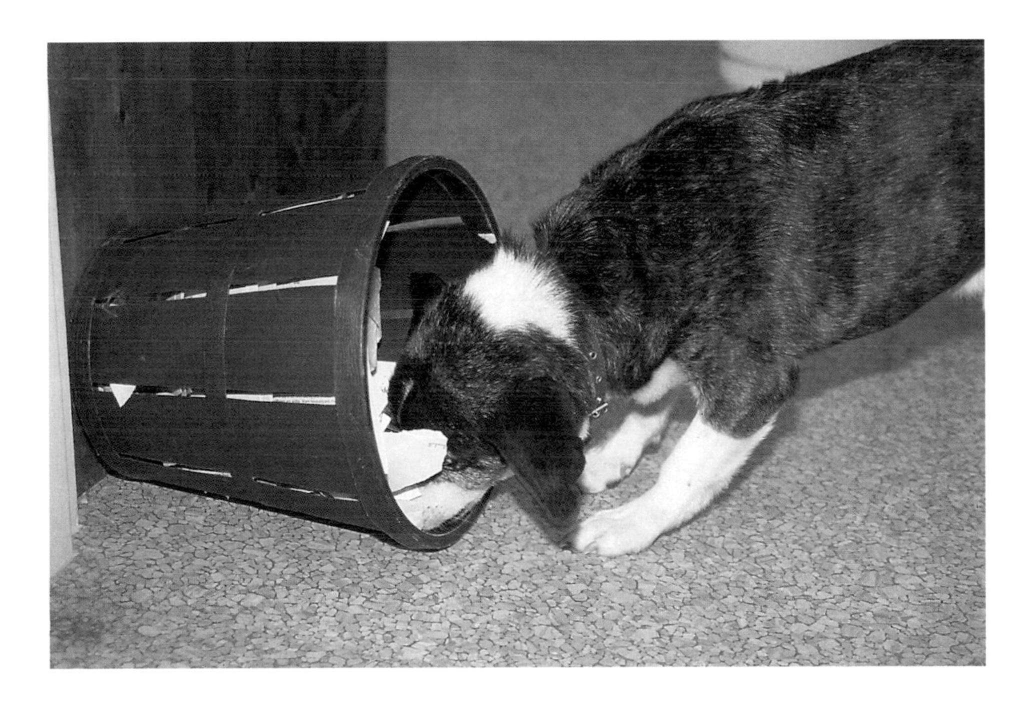

A good scratch or roll in the afternoon sort of rounds out the day . . .

. . . or one can jump on
over to the neighbor's and
see what they're up to . . .

. . . or find a little amusement on the backyard
jungle gym – there's really *so* much to do.

The Labrador retriever is the nation's most popular breed, which means if you spot a big black mutt – one that can fetch – chances are his purebred daddy slipped through an open gate sometime and found his mama.

This isn't at all bad, you see, because of the skills the Lab passed on of grabbing, hauling, fetching, and carrying: the great secret to family longevity – entertainment!

Tip Number Eleven: "No matter what the Boss is doing, follow him or her around and look interested. That way, you come off as intelligent and caring, making you indispensable and one of Life's Great Companions. After all, it isn't as if he's going to ask you to actually do anything."

NO DOGS ALLOWED ON THE BEACH.

Yeah, *right*. Mutts will be where their people are. Besides, there's so much to do, so much to see, and there's the feeling of cool sand between one's toes.

You know, it really has
been a full day.

The Vet

by Steve Smith

Among the experiences a person shares with his dog, walks in the park, maybe a little Sunday-paper fetching, or a little Frisbee in the backyard are the more pleasant ones to come to mind.

Yet, there are other experiences, ones we allow to fleet only briefly across our conscious. These are less than memorable, harrowing for both human and canine. Topping my personal list of these dubious days of dogdom is a visit to the vet.

Now, a dog that can't, after three years of yard training, learn the meanings of the words "come," "sit," and "heel" will learn, after one trip to the pooch health parlor, not only what the word "vet" means, but he will learn to spell it, as in: "Catch the dog because I'm taking him to the v-e-t." Sport vanishes like a snowflake in a campfire.

A dog that has impeccable manners around the house, company, and small children is reduced to the four-footed equivalent of the Hillside Strangler within microseconds of entering the Vet's waiting room. In short, the average dog wants to go to the vet as much as you would look forward to hemorrhoid surgery. So that I will not be accused of making all this up, I have decided to set down in print the latest bout I had with my faithful collie/other stuff, Toby, during a recent trip to the vet. I have recorded all times and events as they happened with no embellishments. See if this doesn't sound like Your typical trip. Since I was busy most of the time, my notes are cryptic at best.

8:45 a.m. – I announce to Wife that it is time for booster shot for Dog. Wife, her left eye starting to twitch, laughs in high pitched, hysterical giggle.

8:47 a.m. – I locate Dog under bed in the spare bedroom, paws wrapped around bed frame and glazed look in his eyes. I must take bed apart to separate Dog from furniture.

9:12 a.m. – Dog and I arrive at Vet's office. Dog holds onto steering wheel as I attempt to remove him from vehicle. I am amazed at strength of this animal and strength of GM steering columns, but disappointed in the strength of new leather leash, which breaks in the scuffle.

9:15 a.m. – We enter Vet's office. I am dragging Dog behind me with remnants of leash. Dog pushes ahead of him three metric tons of gravel from Vet's parking lot. I tell little teenage receptionist that I am here and wait while she pulls Dog's file and places it on desk. I notice that the file is the only one of all those assembled with large black spot in upper right-hand corner. I comment on this, and Receptionist smiles wanly and excuses herself to answer a phone that I could swear wasn't ringing.

9:20 a.m. – Seated in waiting room, I try to read magazine (circa 1948). Dog tries to pick fight with male half of a matched pair of grey French poodles. I separate animals after Dog has shredded hand-knitted sweater that Pierre (for this is the name of the beast) is wearing. I note with some relief that Dog has not tried to perpetrate any ungentlemanly acts upon Fifi, the female half of the poodle tandem.

9:21 a.m. – Dog attempts ungentlemanly act with Fifi. I intervene and get a glass of water for female owner of poodles who apparently suffers from an asthmatic condition.

9:26 a.m. – Dog has suddenly become a model of decorum, resting between my feet on the floor. Decorum has something to do with the recent entrance (at 9:25) of a great Dane with the physical dimensions of large, chest-type freezer. Dane lies at his owner's feet and glares at Dog, who has taken a sudden interest in his toenails.

9:35 a.m. – I enter Vet's examination room, a small, sterile smelling cubicle with one window that looks out onto the parking lot. I wait quietly as Dog eats draperies. Vet enters and asks me to place Dog on slippery, stainless steel examination table. Dog likes this about like I enjoy a root canal. Finally, I catch dog (thanks to small size of room) and place him on table. Vet approaches.

9:38 a.m. – Vet notes that Dog is disgustingly healthy and will no doubt live to relieve himself on both our graves. I am unsure of how I should take this news, as Vet tells me this with no discernible enjoyment. Vet comes at Dog with parvovirus serum in syringe. Dog looks as though the Second Coming has arrived and all the good hiding spots are taken. I grapple with Dog. Vet grapples with Dog. Vet drops syringe. Vet glares at me and Dog. Dog glares back. I turn away and examine what is left of drapes.

9:41 a.m. – Vet has fresh syringe and look of vindication – on his face. Vet injects Dog with technique and enthusiasm normally reserved for serious Olympic javelin competitors. Dog vocally carries on as though an important male appendage is being amputated. I comment on this, and Vet says maybe next time.

9:44 a.m. – Dog and I emerge from examination room and visit teenaged Receptionist who – until this very morning –-had entertained dreams of becoming a vet. I pay bill and leave. As door closes behind me, I hear faint but growing crescendo of applause.

9:54 a.m. – I arrive home and Wife notes that Receptionist has called and I have left remains of leash in waiting room. Vet also told Wife that I needn't return for the leash. He will mail it to me.

Free Puppies

The Accidental Acquisition

Go ahead – you tell her it's "just a mutt."

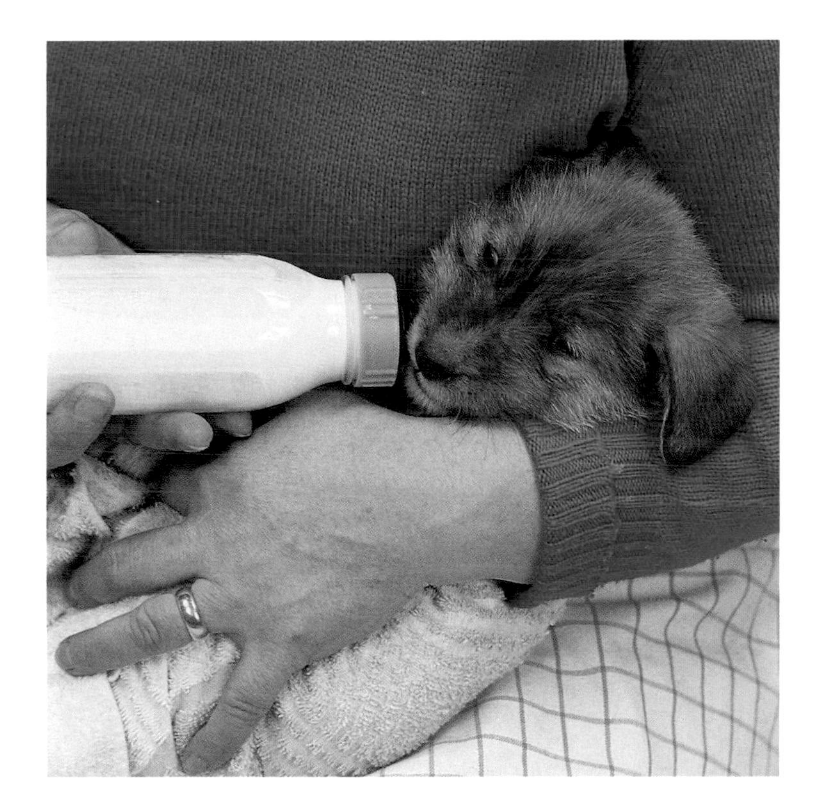

Maybe you see the fateful sign "Free Puppies" alongside the road, or someone gives you the story of, "If you don't take him, he'll have to be destroyed," which of course works. In any event, you went for a nice little ride in the country with your nice little family, and suddenly, somehow, there it is: the furry little mongrel destined to change the course of your life for the next decade and more.

A litter of mutt puppies – a canine three-bean salad. The world is new, and big, and so fascinating.

It is during this time that the lessons of life will be learned, the ones that will place the pup in good standing with whomever he or she catches on with.

The curiosity, the adventuresome ways, the mutt-like comings and goings that will mark the pup as a good, not-so-good, or incorrigible citizen – all of these are learned in those early days of youth, just as they are for us.

On average, a mutt pup will live – barring accident, disease, or just plain bad luck – ten years or longer. And what will he do to fill up the time? Here's a rundown:

• Ruin $1,000 worth of shrubbery, most of it in your neighbor's yard where you can't not replace it (who says you can't use a double negative?).

• Eat three to five pieces of medium-sized furniture ranging from an end table through a couch, but probably not a piano. I had a mutt once by the name of Chum who ate an entire, brand new recliner rocker right down to the imprints the legs left in the rug.

• Ruin at least four christenings/Bar Mitzvahs/birthday parties by mingling with your guests while vomiting up pieces of squirrel.

• Cause to be soiled 650 carpets, or the same carpet 650 times.

• Sleep on sofas, beds, and chairs 3,200 nights while shedding four metric tons of fur.

• Involve you in at least one lawsuit involving a mailman/paper boy/UPS driver/Jehovah's Witness.

• Spit back at you 1,400 heartworm pills. (A dog that couldn't smell a skunk if it moved in with him can smell a heartworm pill inside a piece of weenie smeared with peanut butter tossed to him at forty miles an hour.)

• Cheerfully asked to be scratched behind the ears by the drug addicts burglarizing your home while you're next door planting the new shrubbery you had to buy for the neighbor.

Sadly, there are many who never get beyond those days, never know the joys of adulthood. They never get the chance because they are too legion in number, and there are not enough people willing to give a mutt pup a home, for the numbers are just too overwhelming.

Consider this: Mathematically, one female dog, letting nature chart her course, and given the average size of the resulting litters, and if all the pups survive to breed, will start a process that could produce *67,000* pups in but six years. There are simply not enough homes – let me repeat that: There are simply not enough homes. So people do each day that which they dread doing: They euthanize – kill – unwanted puppies by the thousands. They have to.

Or do they? There is another way and that is the sterilization of females and the neutering of males. A spayed lady mutt brings forth no puppies. Although it's been written and said hundreds of times, sterilization is the only way these animals, in the long run, can survive.

When a dog finally passes on, there is an emptiness, a place in our hearts that will never be filled again in exactly the way it was. Because no matter how many dogs we have over the years, each is unique, a friend, and when they go away, our lives are changed forever in many small ways

When our dog Jess died early last spring, my son, Jake, wrote to me from college. One phrase has stayed with me: "Dogs will always be part of us. A famous line says, 'dogs will die and men will weep for them, so long as there are men and dogs.' There is a price for their love, and that price is the sadness of departure. Friends are never forgotten, and the closer we get to them, the longer they will be with us when they're gone."

Socks

by Steve Smith

When I was in school, I woke up long enough in a psychology class to hear the professor talking about something he called "closure."

Closure, it turns out, is the feeling that a human has for wanting things to be complete; to come full circle. Finished. It is closure that gives you and me fits as we wait for the other shoe to drop, or makes us gnash our teeth when somebody starts writing on a chalkboard without completely erasing it first.

Closure can come along at any time and ease your pain, sometimes years later.

When I was about six or seven, I had a little old mutt puppy named Socks. Socks and I were inseparable buddies for the half year he was with me. He used to sleep at the foot of my bed, and the last thing I felt at night and the first thing I felt again in the morning was his warm, wiggly form. I loved him with a love that has dimmed little as the years have passed.

One day, Socks turned up missing. There was a neighborhood rumor about someone being seen coaxing him into a car, but nothing could ever be proved.

Well, Socks stayed missing, and I cried myself to sleep for a lot of nights. If you've never lost a dog, then you don't know the feeling, but believe me, it only slightly diminishes with time. My parents tried everything to get me to brighten up, with no apparent luck. Maturity and years healed the wound so it no longer festered openly, just sort of scabbed over. Waiting.

One day, years later, the scab broke open. My family and I were visiting my parents at their wooded acreage in northern Michigan when the tagalong family mongrel, Buckshot, turned up missing.

Now, Old Buck is a pretty good hound. He resembles a big, lovable bear cub more than he does a proper dog, and this day he decided to see what was on the other side of the mountain.

The problem is, Chris, who was seven at the time, figured that Buck was his personal property. The other kids were fond of the dog too, but not like Chris.

When he was seven, Chris was the archetypical freckled faced little guy with missing teeth and chubby cheeks. He also had the knack of looking sad and pitiful even when he was happy. When he was broken-hearted, angels held their breath.

Well, Chris figured his pal was gone forever, and looking at him, I could feel the years peel away. I could see myself and Socks all over again. The old pain coming back.

The rain started to fall softly as I hoisted myself into my Jeep and began driving back roads, stopping to call the dog with a disturbing touch of frenzy in my voice. In my mind's eye, I could see Chris back at the cabin, waiting with falling hopes, out in the rain wearing a slicker that was way too big.

Miles later, and with a throat scraped raw from screaming, I still hadn't reduced the family pet to possession. Driving back to the cabin, I parked the Jeep and took off on foot, avoiding Chris' eyes, not wanting to admit that maybe a city-bred dog could get irreparably turned around in all that wilderness.

I struck out for the depths of a quaint little piece of real estate the locals refer to as "Deadman's Swamp," muttering under my breath about dogs and their hold on small boys. If you've ever wandered around alone way back in the woods as nightfall is setting in, then you know what kinds of tricks your mind can play on you. I felt my vision fog up. The old scab was being picked open.

After five miles of walking and screaming and running and sweating, I finally sat down on a slab of rock near an open meadow and tried to sort out how I was going to tell the little man that lived at my house that I couldn't find his dog.

From behind me, I heard a rustle. Whipping around, I saw Old Buck bounding up to me with that where-the-hell-have-you-been attitude that runaway dogs muster up when they're finally found. We rolled on the ground together, my frustration dissolving in the wet ferns. After a bit, I put the dog at heel and we half stumbled and half ran back to the cabin.

When we came out of the woods, my own father, my son with the long face, and the vagabond pooch grabbed and hugged one another. This is when it hit me, this closure.

I felt disembodied; I was suddenly an outsider. More than that, I felt as if I weren't even there at that spot. Instead, I was transported back in time to witness a homecoming I'd hoped for, but never experienced.

My Dad was still there, trim and fit despite his years, and looking 30 again. The little boy hugging the spotted hound was me – a quarter century ago. And Old Buck? He was another, now long-dead beagle who'd finally found his way back.

Socks had come home.

EPILOGUE

Just My Dog

by Gene Hill

He's just my dog.

He is my other eyes that can see above the clouds, my other ears that hear above the winds. He is the part of me that can reach out to sea.

He has told me a thousand times over that I am his reason for being – by the way he rests against my leg; by the way he thumps his tail at my smallest smile; by the way he shows his hurt when I leave without taking him – I think it makes him sick with worry when he is not along to care for me.

When I am wrong, he is delighted to forgive. When I am angry, he clowns to make me smile. When I am happy, he is joy unbounded.

When I am a fool, he ignores it. When I succeed, he brags.

Without him, I am only another man. With him, I am all powerful.

He is loyalty itself. He has taught me the meaning of devotion.

With him, I know a secret comfort and a private peace. He has brought me understanding where before I was ignorant.

His head on my knee can heal human hurts. His presence by my side is protection against my fears of dark and unknown things. He has promised to wait for me – whenever, wherever – in case I need him. And I expect I will, as I always have.

He's just my dog.

Century
NOTICE
TO ALL
DOGS
NO · ABSOLUTLY NO
LEG · LIFTING
ON LEFT REAR
(THAT'S MY SPOT)